**WHY DO WE
SAY THAT?**

WHY DO WE SAY THAT?

An Exercise in Etymology

Origins of Words and Phrases in Common Use in the English Language

Noel P. Crighton

with illustrations by Tony Grogan

Human & Rousseau
Cape Town   Pretoria   Johannesburg

First impression 1997
Second impression 1998

Copyright © 1997 by Noel P. Crighton
First edition in 1997 by Human & Rousseau
State House, 3-9 Rose Street, Cape Town
Cover illustration by Tony Grogan
Cover design by Annelize van Rooyen
Typography by Anna-Marie Spies
Typeset in 11 on 13 pt Plantin by Human & Rousseau, Cape Town
Printed and bound by National Book Printers
Drukkery Street, Goodwood, Western Cape

ISBN 0 7981 3743 6

No part of this book may be reproduced or transmitted in any
form or by any means, electronic or mechanical, or by
photocopying, recording or microfilming, or stored in any
retrieval system, without the written permission of the publisher

PREFACE

Doubtless it is stating the obvious to say that the English language is a most complex one. It probably has the biggest dictionary in the world and, for a foreigner, endeavouring to master the contradictions and illogicalities of English, must be an uphill task. The subtle nuances – same word, different meaning, same pronunciation, different word – is often confusing.

This book will be of no use whatsoever to the foreign student! It aims to entertain, and at the same time surprise, many people with the explanation of how a particular word or expression, taken for granted in everyday conversation, came into being. We seldom question the origins of our rich turn of phrase until a child asks, 'Why do we say that?' I shouldn't think many of you have wondered why the wedding trip of a newlywed couple is called a honeymoon – or why the person illicitly listening to your conversation is an *eavesdropper*, or why one takes *a busman's holiday* or *passes the buck* ...

It is hoped this little book will fire your interest in etymology. What a dry sounding word, but what a fascinating subject! I feel confident that, as you browse through the book, you will find every word and phrase familiar, yet be surprised at how far back in history they have their origins, often sinister origins. Look, for instance, at *pulling your leg* and *gone West*.

I have always loved words and grew up in an era before electronic gadgets distracted one from the joys of a good book. I come from the UK and during the 1970s was one of a team of twelve speakers covering the British Isles for KWV, giving talks on the history of Cape wines and conducting wine tastings. At the same time I studied for the Guild of Sommeliers (wine butlers).

It was during these studies that I discovered that wine and

ale gave rise to *honeymoon* and *taken down a peg or two*. This roused my interest in word and phrase origins and led me to research into etymology for many years.

I would like to give credit to all the many books I studied. I can't! From the shelves of public libraries, several encyclopaedias and many a dusty tome found in a second-hand book shop, I gathered the contents of this book.

Enjoy it!

Noel P. Crighton
Hermanus, 1997

A

A-1 When we want to say something is the best – first rate – we sometimes use the term A-1. This is derived from Lloyd's Register of Shipping when applied to ships in first-class condition. Lloyd's of London insure ships throughout the world and those with an A-1 rating attract favourable rates. The 'A' denotes either new or restored vessels and the figure 1 or 2 the excellence of the ship's stores.

ACE IN THE HOLE Describes a strategy in stud poker whereby a player turns an ace face down on the table and is the only one who knows he has a secret source of unmatchable power. The term is now generally applied to a good move, argument or manoeuvre kept in reserve for use at a strategic time.

ACHILLES HEEL In Greek mythology Thetis, the leader of the sea nymphs, wanted to make sure that her infant son Achilles would be invulnerable in battle as an adult. She held him by the heel and dipped him into the River Styx, whose water was believed to confer invulnerability, but his heel remained dry where her hand was cupped over it. Achilles died as a result of a wound from an arrow that struck him in that heel. Thus we often refer to a weak spot in an otherwise strong character or position as his/her *Achilles heel*.

ACID TEST In times when gold was in wide circulation, the question often arose as to whether an alleged gold coin or object was genuine. Nitric acid was applied. If the piece was false, the acid decomposed the metal, but if it was genuine, the gold remained intact. A crucial or severe test of quality.

AFTERMATH 'Math' is grass that has been mowed and dried to hay. If a second crop of grass is cut for hay, it is known as *aftermath*. Now the word is in common usage to mean anything happening after the main event.

ALL BALLSED-UP There is nothing crude in this description of a messy situation. First recorded last century, it applied to horses working in snow, which gradually built up to balls of ice in their hooves. This effectively put the poor animals on skates – especially on cobbled surfaces – causing them to fall.

ALOOF Maritime terms have produced many words and sayings which we use freely these days – most of them coming from the complex days of sailing. The Dutch naval command *a loef* directed a helmsman either to steer further away from the shore or to the windward side of another vessel. Since both involved moving away from something, the term entered general parlance as *aloof*.

On the same theme, a ship which anchored outside the harbour, was said to 'stand-off', hence *stand-offish*. Also, the span of water visible from the shore is called the 'offing' so any ship approaching the harbour was said to be *in the offing*.

THE APPLE OF HIS EYE In Old English the eye's pupil was known as an apple because it was thought to be spherical and solid. Since the pupil is a crucial and indispensable portion of the eye, it serves as a symbol of something cherished. It appears in part of a song by Moses:

> 'He found him in a desert land,
> and in the howling waste of the wilderness;
> he encircled him, he cared for him,
> he kept him as *the apple of his eye*.'

ASSASSIN Moslem fanatics in the eleventh century used to wind themselves up on hashish before they went on their drug-crazed killings. *Hashshashin* meant 'he who eats hashish' and this eventually became *assassin*.

ATLAS In 1595 Rumold Mercator published a nicely bound special edition of his father's maps. Wanting an impressive cover design, he chose a picture of *Atlas* on one knee with the world on his shoulders. Not only did this secure the myth of *Atlas* sentenced to carry the world on his back, it established his name forever for a book of maps.

B

BAKER'S DOZEN In 1266 an Act of Parliament in England laid down standards of weight for bread. In order to make certain they were meeting the standard, bakers adopted the practice of giving thirteen loaves to vendors for each dozen they bought. This became known as a *baker's dozen*.

BALLOON In World War I, when troops crouched in their trenches waiting for the order to charge across No Man's Land towards the enemy, the first they knew of impending battle was when observation balloons were winched into the sky to direct artillery fire in the softening-up process. They would mutter that *the balloon has gone up*, an expression we use now to mean the action, or trouble, has begun. Once ordered to charge they would scramble over the parapets and rush forward screaming blue murder. They had *gone over the top*, giving us another common saying.

BANK In medieval Italy money-lenders operated from a bench in the market square. The Italian for bench is *banco* and from this we get our present *bank*. If a money-lender became insolvent, public officials smashed his bench and put up notices that the trader had been declared *bancorotto*, or 'broken bench' – which gives us *bankrupt*.

The old Dutch business establishment had an expression for a person gone broke: *to goe, to de dogs*, meaning 'money gone, credit gone' and it is easy to see where we get our present saying *gone to the dogs*.

BARKING UP THE WRONG TREE Hunting raccoons was popular in the USA in the 19th century. Because the animals are nocturnal, hunters took dogs to help find them. The

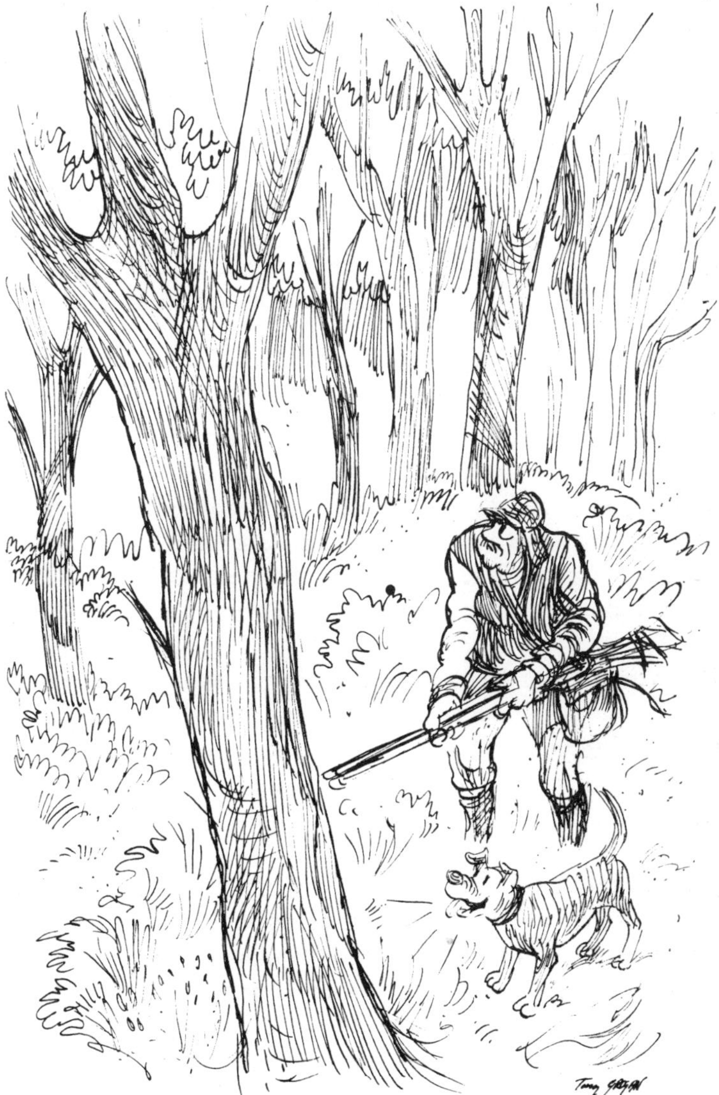

pursued raccoon was likely to take to a tree and the dog was supposed to lurk at the base of that tree and bark until the hunter arrived. But if the dog was *barking up the wrong tree* the hunter was unlikely to get his prey.

BARREL   In the days of sail pork was pretty much a standard ration, stored on board in barrels sealed with a lining of fat. When adverse weather caused ships to be overdue at their next port of call food was sometimes in very short supply and many sailors were driven to rooting in the fat of discarded barrels for any scraps of meat adhering to the undersides of the fat. This gave rise to the term *scraping the bottom of the barrel*.

BARMY   In early distilleries the scum that formed on top of the fermented liquid was know as 'barm'. Anyone stupid enough to sup this scum was called *barmy*.

BECK AND CALL   In 1470 the Earl of Worcester ordered that servants should be at his *beck and call*. A beck was a nod of the head or crooking of a finger, but if the servant failed to see this, the master might have to call.

BERSERK   goes back to the days of the Vikings. They were a savage people who ran amok in many countries. Many wore bearskins (*bjorn sekr*) and others were stark naked – *berr sekr* or 'bare of shirt'. This is the origin of any irrational or violent behaviour we now call going *berserk*.

BEST BIB AND TUCKER   In the 17th century, important banquets called for the wearing of one's *best bib and tucker*. In those days, people wore heavy padded clothing that was impossible to wash and, when eating, the women wore *tuckers* – a variant of 'tugger' – describing the way they were removed – to protect their clothing. Men wore *bibs*, a name derived from the Latin *bibere*, to drink – because they were more likely to slop ale down their doublets. Nearly 300 years later, we still use the expression.

BEST FOOT FORWARD There was an old superstition that the left-hand side of the body brought bad luck. This belief required that a safe journey would be achieved by stepping off with the right foot first. We still talk of putting our *best foot forward*.

This belief that the forces of evil prevailed on the left side of the body dictated that one should not get up from the left side of the bed or put one's left foot on the floor first. Innkeepers sometimes put the left side of the bed against the wall to protect guests from this hazard. When it's a bad day and nothing seems to go right, we still unwittingly invoke this superstition by saying one must have *got out of the wrong side of the bed*.

BEYOND THE PALE In Roman times areas of civilisation, law and order were marked with stakes. The Latin for these stakes was *palus*. This system of marking was carried through to the Middle Ages in Britain, and in the 14th century there was an English settlement just outside Dublin. By then *palus* had been anglicised to 'pale' and anyone living outside the demarcated area was said to be living *beyond the pale*.

BIBLE In ancient times papyrus was one of the materials used for writing on – easy to see where the word 'paper' comes from. The Greeks called papyrus *Byblos* and when books were first written, they were known as *Biblia*. As the writings or the *Bible* were first called 'The Books', and written on papyrus, the word *Bible* developed.

In addition to papyrus, another early material was a wooden block on which letters were scratched. These blocks were made from beech, known to the Anglo-Saxons as 'boc'. From this comes our word *book*.

BINT The British army used – and abused – many foreign words. *Bint* is the Arabic for daughter, but amongst the soldiery it became a derogatory term for a woman. Also Arabic, the beggars' cry of *bakshee* for alms became *buckshee* to the British, who used it to describe anything given for free.

BLACKBALLED Many exclusive clubs insist that a proposed new member must be unanimously accepted by all existing members. To preserve anonymity voting is carried out by the use of white and black balls. Let one black ball appear and that applicant will not be granted membership. He has been *blackballed*.

BLACKJACK The tavern maid of Merrie England, like the barmaid of today, was always prone to molestation by someone in his cups. As the maid moved about the inn replenishing tankards, she carried heavy leather jugs stiffened with pitch, and she wasn't above administering an instant headache to the unruly with one of the jugs. The jugs earned the name *blackjack* and eventually coshes of all sorts came to be so called.

BLACKMAIL In the 16th century absentee English landlords owned many farms in Scotland and the tenant farmers paid their rent – known in those parts as 'mail' – in the form of either 'white mail', which was silver money, or 'black mail' which was produce or livestock.

Some poor farmers, unable to raise the required cash, were often unscrupulously exploited by their landlords and forced to hand over much more in goods than they would have paid in cash. Thus they were *blackmailed*, a term now generally used when money is obtained by threats of some sort, often relating to information the victim would prefer not to have made public.

BLACK MARIA In my young days as a policeman in Britain we used to drive black patrol cars, which were always called *Black Marias*. But why Maria? The name comes from the US city of Boston where, in the 19th century, a huge and ultra-strong negress ran a lodging house. She was always known as Black Maria and the local police often sent for her when dealing with violent prisoners. None would dream of opposing her when she loomed up, collared them and marched them to the waiting prison van or lock-up.

BLESS YOU The ancients believed that any violent exhalation would cause the eviction of the soul. Thus, anyone sneezing was *blessed* as he was thought to be in mortal danger. Nor was it politeness that prompted people to cover their mouths when yawning. The gesture was intended to keep the soul in and evil spirits out.

BLOODHOUNDS Not so called because of their extensive use in tracking people, but because they were the first breed to have records kept of their bloodline. The monks of St. Hubert began keeping pedigree details in France in the ninth century.

BLOW HOT AND COLD This well-known saying comes from Aesop's fables, which tell of a satyr meeting a cold and starving traveller in the forest. The satyr invites him to his cave and notices on the way that the traveller keeps blowing on his hands. When asked why, the traveller explains that he is trying to warm his frozen hands. In the cave the satyr gives him a bowl of piping hot gruel and the hungry traveller blows on it. Again he explains why to the satyr, who cries in alarm: 'Be off with you, I'll have no part with a man who can *blow hot and cold* from the same mouth.'

BLUE BLOOD   Commonly used to identify one born to royalty or the aristocracy. The term originates from the period when the dark-skinned Moors ruled Spain. Members of the old Castilian families were wont to say with pride that their blood had not been contaminated by Moorish or other foreign bloods. The term they used of themselves was *sangre azul*, literally 'blue blood', which probably sprang from the fact that the veins of the fair-skinned are visibly blue.

BOB   In the late 1880s Robert Gascoyne-Cecil, third Marquis of Salisbury, had great influence in government. He ensured that his favourite nephew, Arthur Balfour, got some of the best ministerial posts going. Thus giving rise to the saying *Bob's your uncle* for anything easy to do or acquire.

BONES   Early dice were made from animal bones and people using Black American slang said that they were "making bones" when they cavorted and mutterd imprecations at the dice before throwing them. The more experienced, or perhaps cynical, players knew that no amount of blowing or invocations would make the slightest bit of difference as to how the dice fell and so they just picked them up and threw them, *making no bones about it*.

BRIDEGROOM   In bygone days a man who performed humble duties around the house and outbuildings was called a groom (and still is at riding stables). Also, in yesteryears, wedding ceremonies were very lavish affairs and the celebrations could last for several days, during which the husband was expected to wait on his bride hand and foot. In this way he assumed the duties of a manservant, or groom, and became known as the bride's groom, nowadays *bridegroom*.

BRIDESMAID   Our ancestors believed that evil spirits present at a wedding would attempt to disrupt the ceremony by getting at the bride. To confuse these spirits the bride was attended by a group of girls identically dressed and veiled. This feminine entourage survives as the modern *bridesmaid*.

BRASS TACKS   In times gone by, stores selling cloth by the yard measured precise lengths by using brass-headed tacks embedded in their counters. This way, by *getting down to brass tacks*, buyer and seller accurately established the required length of the material.

BROACH   first applied to the pegs used to tap a barrel to allow its contents to flow – hence to *broach a subject*. The word later described heavy metal skewers which were used to turn meat over an open fire. When items of jewellery with skewer-like fastenings first put in an appearance, they were given the same name, but the spelling has now changed to brooch.

The word *broker* also originates from 'broacher' and was applied to a retailer of wine who broached – or tapped – wineskins or casks. He had nothing to do with the production or casking of the wine, but merely bought it wholesale and sold it retail. In other words, he was a middleman and today a 'broker' is a middleman in financial affairs. I do not venture to explain 'pawnbroker'!

BUCKET   For hundreds of years persons bent on committing suicide have stood on a bucket, put a rope over a beam and then round their necks and *kicked the bucket*.

BUNK   The US member of Congress for Buncombe in North Carolina insisted he must 'make a speech for Buncombe'. His lengthy address was rambling and incoherent and he was taken to task for wasting time. Subsequently, any such speech became known as *bunkum* now generally shortened to *bunk*. In other words, a right load of rubbish!

BURTON In World War II members of the RAF favoured the strong, dark ale known as Burton. If a flyer went down into the sea – the 'drink', missing and presumed dead, he was said to have *gone for a burton*, a term now frequently used for anyone or anything knocked over and damaged, often beyond repair.

BUSMAN'S HOLIDAY In the days of horse-drawn buses in London, drivers became very attached to their horses. On their days off they would often ride with the passengers to make sure that the substitute driver was taking good care of the horse. From this we get the expression *a busman's holiday*, used to describe holidays or free time spent doing exactly what a person would do at work.

BUTTONHOLE When we detain, or *buttonhole*, someone to get their ear, we should, strictly speaking, say 'buttonhold'. That was how, in Regency times, a person was detained for a telling off – by holding on to a button.

C

CAMERA From the Latin, meaning a vaulted room or chamber. In such rooms many secret meetings took place. Hence our present expression *in camera* for a meeting from which the press and public are excluded.

CANDLE In the days when people played cards or dice games by candlelight they sometimes paid a nonplayer to hold the candle so that the light fell on the game rather than in the eyes of the players. They also had to pay for the candles. A player having a run of bad luck might well remark that *the game is not worth the candle*. Nowadays we use the expression to describe any activity or arrangement which doesn't repay the time, or money, or effort expended on it.

CAT In the 19th century one cruel form of physical punishment was to flay the wrongdoer with the 'cat-o-nine-tails', a hide whip with nine flails. The very anticipation of this barbarous beating often reduced the victim to terrified silence. From this comes the saying *Has the cat got your tongue?*

This form of punishment was most common on board naval vessels. The crews lived in extremely cramped conditions below decks and the whipping always took place on deck, because below there was literally *not enough room to swing a cat*.

CENOTAPH In ancient Greece, if a person drowned and his body was not recovered, it was the custom to erect a monument called *kenos* (empty) *taphos* (tomb) and from this is derived *cenotaph*.

CHAP The archaic 'chapman' meant a merchant or trader,

usually the forerunner of our present-day barrow boy or street trader, and meant that his goods were 'cheap'. A customer of this chapman was known as a *chap* which, by the 18th century, came to be accepted as a man. The word is still slightly slangy, but frequently used in friendly terms such as 'there's a good chap'.

CHECKMATE   In chess many of the terms come from India – where the game originated over a thousand years ago – and Persia, where it became very popular. The announcement of victory is *checkmate*, which originates from the Persian *shar mat* – 'the king is dead'.

CHOCK-A-BLOCK   In the days of sail no ship could function without the aid of the block and tackle, which did everything from raising and lowering the sails to loading and unloading cargo. When all the hoisting capacity on the rope had been exploited, the block came hard up against the chock. Things were then crammed in tight, or *chock-a-block*.

To free the device it was necessary to pass the rope back through the pulley eyes in the block and back-haul to separate the components. This was called *overhauling* and now refers to any piece of equipment taken apart to effect repair.

CHRISTMAS TREE   In the ninth century the barbaric Hun worshipped trees, believing them to be manifestations of the Earth's life force. When St. Boniface went to try and teach the Teutonic hordes the error of their ways, he found he was unable to break them of this habit. So, on the principal of 'if you can't beat 'em, join 'em' Christian missionaries absorbed the ritual and the Christmas tree came to represent the life force of Christ.

CIGARETTE   The superstition that it is bad luck to *light three cigarettes with one match* has a strong basis in truth. During the Boer War British troops bivouacked for the night would pass round the fags. The flare of the match might attract the attention of a Boer sniper. In the time it took to pass the match to the second man he had lined up his sights. The third one copped it!

CLAPTRAP The theatre employed many strategies to ensnare or bribe audiences into applauding even the poorest of shows and they called these gambits *claptrap*.

CLEAN AS A WHISTLE indicates shining cleanliness of a person or of an object. In the 1800s whistles were used extensively and were mostly made of wood. To be effective they had to be kept very clean.

COASTER Why do we call those rather crude plastic or cardboard mats that go under a glass a *coaster*? At one time these were beautifully embroidered lace or linen affairs that fitted over the base of decanters. In those days tables were deeply polished, quality furniture, not covered with a tablecloth, and the coasters protected the cut-glass decanters from scratching the wood. At the end of a meal the decanters were 'coasted' from one to another around the table. Hence the name *coaster*.

COCK-A-HOOP In fairgrounds of old ale flowed freely. When everything was in full swing, the wooden pegs – or cocks – blocking the air-bleed holes in the beer barrels would be knocked out and placed on one of the metal hoops of the barrel. This enabled the beer to flow unhindered and everybody got truly *cock-a-hoop*.

COCK-AND-BULL We all know this is a story that is a load of old rubbish and usually a pack of lies. There are several versions of how this expression came about. One is based on an old story of a cock and a bull conversing to each other in human language. Since people knew this was impossible they labelled any far-fetched yarn as a 'cock and bull story'.

The version I prefer features the East End of London in Victorian times, where the Cock Tavern became a famous venue for the telling of outrageous stories alleged to be fact.

Listeners wanting to make a name for themselves would carry these yarns to the Bull Inn at the other end of the street, doubtless embellishing it as they wended their way. A *cock-and-bull story*.

COMPANION The Latin for bread is *panis*. The middle part of 'companion' is taken from this and literally means someone you share your bread with.

CONFETTI Italian for sweets, which were thrown during carnivals. In ancient times rice, wheat or nuts were thrown over a bridal couple as a fertility rite to ensure the prosperity and fruitfulness of their marriage. In the 19th century this custom was merged with the throwing of sweets (confetti) and these sweets were subsequently replaced by colourful pieces of paper which retained the name *confetti*.

CORNY The word is American slang, originally used to describe second-rate shows forced to tour rural areas where the 'corn-fed' audiences were less demanding than those on Broadway. Blacked-up minstrel shows of the day provided another theatrical term. Because ham fat was used extensively to remove the heavy black make-up, the performers became known as *ham actors*.

COVENTRY During the Civil War many Royalist soldiers occupied the town and this was bitterly resented by the townsfolk. They forbade anyone fraternising with the military and any girl so caught had her head shaved. Amongst the soldiers this became *sent to Coventry* and is still used to this day when a person is ostracised.

CROCODILE It was formerly believed that the crocodile wept and moaned to attract the sympathetic and helpful – then ate them! In the 1600s a traveller wrote: 'It is the nature of crocodiles, when he would have his prey, to cry and sob – to provoke them to come to him, and then he snatcheth at them.' So the crocodile became a symbol of hypocrisy and

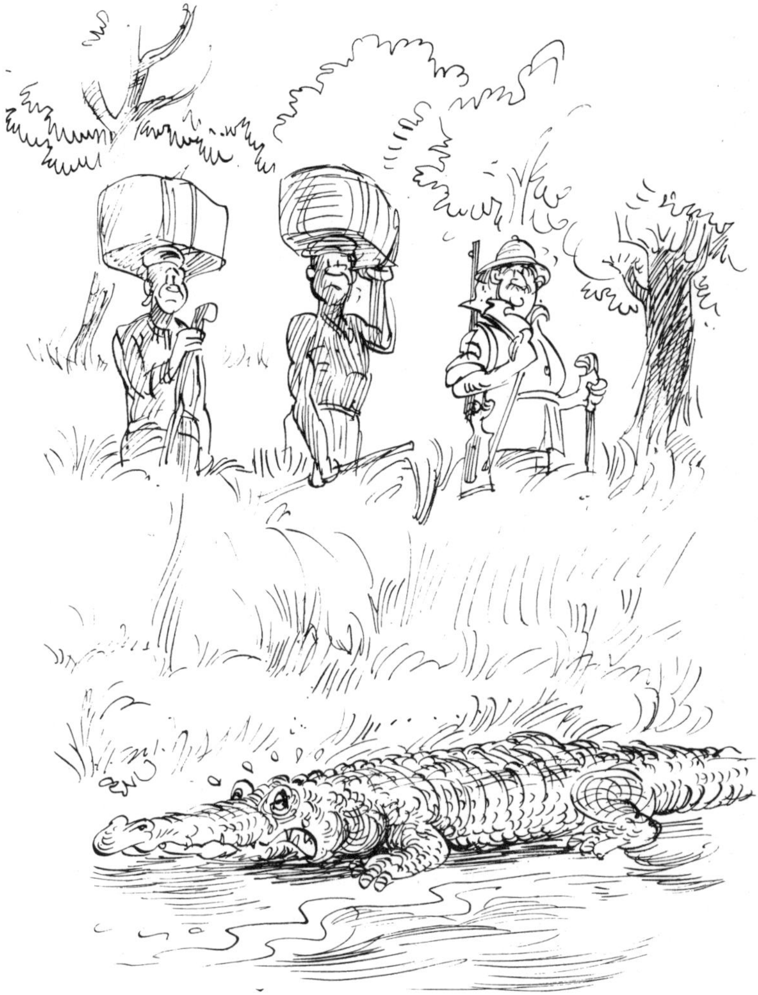

treachery, playing on our pity with false, or *crocodile tears*.

CUBBYHOLE In the Middle Ages young animals were far too precious to be left out at night and were therefore brought into the dwelling. There was usually a warm little recess for these frail young and this was called a *cubbyhole* – or a place for the cubs.

CURFEW Medieval houses were insubstantial buildings, made of wood and thatch and huddled close together. Fireplaces were in the centre of the room and smoke escaped through a hole in the roof. The risk of fire was great and a law was enforced throughout Europe that these open fires should either be extinguished or covered with a lid at eight in the evening. The law was called *couvre-feu*, French for 'cover fire' and a bell was rung in every town at 8 pm to enforce this. As the years passed this rule became identified with the bell itself and the word gradually altered to *curfew*.

D

DAWN When something finally becomes apparent it is as if a light has arrived in the mind. This has been likened to the glimmerings of sunrise, hence *it has dawned on me*.

DAYS The days of the week got their names as follows: *Sunday* for the sun, *Monday* for the moon, *Tuesday* for Tiu, son of Wodin – the Scandinavian God of War, *Wednesday* for Wodin and originally called Wodinsday, *Thursday* for Thor, God of Thunder, *Friday* for Frigg – wife of Odin and Goddess of Love and *Saturday* for the God of Saturn.

Incidentally, in times past, time was counted by nights, not days, hence *fortnight* – or fourteen nights.

AS DEAD AS . . . In times gone by it was frequently the practice to decorate a door with large-headed nails and these can be seen to this day on the doors of old churches, inns and cottages in Europe. Because such nails were totally inanimate and unresponsive, persons who were completely without ideas or prospects of success were likened to these nails and said to be *as dead as a doornail*.

And for people and animals who literally are dead, we use *as dead as a dodo*, referring to the long extinct (and incredibly stupid!) flightless bird.

DEATH In early days dogs were carrion eaters and became associated with death in mythology. The underworlds of all beliefs are guarded by hideous dogs. In Celtic religions this hound was named 'Dormath', which translates to *death's door*, an expression now used to imply the brink of death.

Judas Iscariot told Jesus' enemies that at what is now called the Last Supper he would kiss Jesus to identify him so that he could be arrested and put to death. This is the very obvious origin of *the kiss of death*.

DELIRIOUS describes the condition when your mind is wandering – for instance, when you are seriously ill with fever. Literally, however, you are 'wandering from the furrow'. The Latin word *lira* means furrow, so 'de-lirious' comes from an image of erratic steering when ploughing!

DEN OF THIEVES A place where one has to be on one's guard against a gathering of rogues. When Matthew tells how Jesus drove the money changers and others out of the temple, he reports (21:13) that Jesus "said unto them, it is written, my house shall be called the house of prayer but ye have made it a den of thieves".

DIAMOND A diamond as it comes from the mine, needs cutting and polishing. A person who is unpolished and inexperienced, but nevertheless shows promise in some field, or whose heart is in the right place despite his rough exterior, is sometimes said to be *a rough diamond*.

DISASTER The Latin for star is *astrum*. Add the negative prefix *dis* and it means an occasion when the stars are unfavourable. Hence *disaster*.

DONKEY'S YEARS Donkeys do not, in fact, live for many years. The expression *donkey's years* is a corruption of 'donkey's ears', because of their length.

DOWN IN THE MOUTH A person suffering disappointment, or in low spirits, will often turn down the corners of the mouth. Hence the expression.

DRAB In the Middle Ages a simple woollen cloth of a nondescript yellowy colour was used by the peasants to make clothing. This cloth was called *drab* and the name gradually came to apply to anything rather dreary. Later the cloth itself became 'drap' and from this we get *draper*.

DYED-IN-THE-WOOL is a very old English term for something deeply ingrained. It is based on the fact that dyes applied to raw wool are more lasting than those that are applied after the wool has been spun into thread and woven into cloth. So anything that is *dyed-in-the-wool* is basic, fixed, unremovable.

E

EATING If you have a tame and trusting animal it will often take food from your hand. We now apply the term eating out of your (or my) hand to a very cooperative or submissive person who will do anything one asks of them.

While on the subject of eating, did you know that the English language does not have a single native word to describe an eating establishment? 'Restaurant' and 'café' are French; 'canteen' and 'cafeteria' are of Spanish-American origin.

EARMARKED If we set aside something to be used for a specific requirement we often say it has been *earmarked* for that purpose. It comes from farm animals having their ears tabbed or daubed with a dye to identify ownership.

EASEL Many readers will remember blackboard and easel, but where does the word *easel* come from? It originates from the Dutch 'ezel' – an ass or donkey. This animal patiently bears its load. So does the easel. A similar logic gives us 'clotheshorse' which stands equally patiently whilst your clothes dry on it.

EASTER A number of Christian festivals and customs have their roots in primitive early belief and *Easter* is no exception. Despite its very Christian significance the name originally came from the pagan Goddess Eastre, the Anglo-Saxon Goddess of the Dawn, who was specially honoured at the Spring Equinox at a great festival called *Eastron*.

EAVESDROPPER Have you ever wondered why a person who listens in on your conversation is so called? The saying goes back to medieval times when houses had thatched roofs but no guttering. The roofs hung out over the building to protect the walls from falling water, and the law required that there was sufficient space between houses to prevent drainage from one house falling onto another. The overhang was originally called an 'eavesdrip', which gradually became 'eavesdrop'. The word *eavesdropper* was derived in the 15th century to denote a nosy person who lurked under the eavesdrop.

ECHO Greek mythology tells of a nymph who never stopped talking. It got so bad that the Goddess Hera punished her by depriving her of the power of speech – except to repeat the last words of others. The nymph's name was *Echo*. Got it?

EENY, MEENY, MINY, MO When children – and sometimes adults – want to select something and are spoilt for choice they often chant *eeny, meeny, miny, mo*. This saying has quite a sinister past. It is a corruption of Druid numbers one, two, three and four, which were used to make a random selection for ritual sacrifice.

EGG Due to the shape of an egg it is often linked with zero. The American expression to describe failure or flop is *laying an egg*. Our cricket expression *out for a duck* originates from the shortening of 'out for a duck's egg'.

Similarly a zero score in tennis is *love* – a slurring of the French *l'oeuf* (egg).

F

FACE THE MUSIC There are two sources to the origins of this expression. Firstly, it refers to a very nervous actor going on stage before both the audience and the pit orchestra – the music.

Secondly, in the army of the past a soldier dismissed from his regiment often had to hear the band playing the 'Rogue's March' as he was marched away. Now, of course, we use the expression in relation to confronting or coping with a difficult situation.

FASCIST The *fasces* in ancient Rome was a bundle of long birch rods tied together with red straps, and with an axe head sticking out to denote that the carrier had power over life and death. Carriers preceded officials entitled to the *fasces* and the number of carriers indicated the man's status in high office.

When Benito Mussolini founded his Italian Movement in 1919 he resurrected the *fasces* as his own symbol and named his political party after it – the *Fascists*.

FAT LADY In America during World War II, a lady called Kate Smith became famous for singing 'God Bless America' at the end of important national functions. She was a lady of considerable proportions, with a very powerful singing voice, and as the song always signalled the end of an event she gave rise to the saying that something's *not over till the fat lady sings*.

FEATHER Long ago it was the custom in many countries to award a feather to a soldier who had killed an enemy. This feather was worn in his helmet or some other type of headgear. It was an honour in recognition of his achievement. It was *a feather in his cap*.

FINGERS There was an old superstition that making the sign of the cross wards off danger and evil. This is the probable origin of *keeping one's fingers crossed* for luck.

FLASH The old flintlock musket was a complicated affair. The ball had to be rammed down the barrel and the gunpowder inserted into the pan. A spark had to come from the flint to ignite the powder, which in turn propelled the ball towards its target. Sometimes the powder went off, but the ball didn't move. This was called *a flash in the pan* and modern use of the expression refers to a temporary success or attraction.

FLOG In times gone by, seamen signing on to crew a ship were paid up-front for a stated period. Their term for this period was 'dead horse', and until such time had passed they saw no sense in doing more than was required of them because they would not get a penny more. So why *flog a dead horse*?

FLOTSAM AND JETSAM is a term gradually dying out in our language. I doubt if many younger persons would know what it meant: odds and ends or items of little value. Often used now in a derogatory sense, both words come from maritime law.

Flotsam refers to goods found floating in the sea (usually as a result of a shipwreck) and jetsam applies to items thrown overboard, often to lighten the load in dangerous conditions. The modern use of the word *jettison* originates from jetsam.

FLYING COLOURS Triumphantly, proudly. The colours are the flags or banners borne by a naval ship or military unit. In victory the colours remain prominently displayed, in defeat they are lowered.

And so, today, gaining success in a testing situation is to *come through with flying colours*.

FRAME In the criminal world, to *frame* somebody now means either someone has quietly snitched to the police or evidence has been fabricated to ensure a conviction. But originally, the term came from 'to dance in the sheriff's picture frame' – a macabre reference to the gallows.

The person who snitched is known as a *stool pigeon* and this comes from when a captive pigeon was tied to a stool and moved about to entice other pigeons into the range of the hunter's gun.

FREELANCE 'Free companies' of lancers in medieval times referred to discharged soldiers who offered themselves as mercenaries for any casual war or plundering exploit. Now, of course, the word *freelance* means anyone, particularly journalists, owing no particular allegiance and prepared to work for the highest bidder.

FRISBEE In 1871 William Russell Frisbee set up the Frisbee Pie Company in Bridgeport, Connecticut. Nearby was a college that eventually became Yale University. The students of this college not only enjoyed the pies, but found that the stiff paper plates were ideal for throwing discus-style across the campus.

In 1948 Frederick Morrison, a former student of Yale – where they were still eating the pies and lobbing the plates about – produced the first plastic replicas that became the popular toy of today.

FROG A widely held belief in Merrie England was that great danger existed in the drinking of water from still ponds because of the presence of frogspawn. If ingested, this was believed to mature in the human stomach to produce live frogs, which would then attempt to escape through the mouth. This is the source of the expression *to have a frog in the throat*.

FULL TILT At the medieval joust the knights carried a very heavy lance in a vertical position. As he galloped towards his adversary, the rider gradually lowered the lance to line up on his target. By the time the lance had been fully tilted the horse was going at full gallop. Thus the knight was going *full tilt*.

FUNNY BONE If you bang the tip of your elbow – where the ulnar nerve is close to the surface – you say, often in agony, you've banged your *funny bone*. The upper arm is anatomically called the humerus. You may not find it funny, but everyone else does!

G

GARNISH The word instantly brings culinary matters to mind but, in medieval times, the word meant 'to warn' and, in particular, to alert a town of impending attack. Once the warning had been given, the battlements bristled with the paraphernalia of defensive weapons and the fortifications then stood 'garnished'.

GETS MY GOAT Annoys severely. The expression came from the practice of some horse trainers putting a goat in the stall with a nervous horse to soothe it. If someone, wanting to see the horse lose a race, came and took the goat away, the horse would presumably succumb to an attack of nerves and would not run well. One could imagine the trainer being severely annoyed if someone *got his goat*.

GOODBYE Did you know that this is a prayer compressed into one word? It is a shortened version of 'God be with you'.

GOOSEBERRY The modern interpretation of the expression *playing gooseberry*, whereby a third party is present to spoil the fun of a couple, is somewhat a reverse of its original meaning. In Old England, courting couples had to have a chaperone and it was a lucky pair of lovers who had an understanding chaperone, happy to wander off and pick gooseberries for a while.

GRAIN It goes against a craftsman's instincts, as well as being hard work and illogical, to plane a piece of wood against the grain. Hence the saying *it goes against the grain* when you do something that you know shouldn't be done that way.

GUM UP In the 19th century, lubrication of machinery was more of an art than a science and the oil sometimes got so gummy that it interfered with, rather than aided, the smooth operation of the machine. These days, if an undertaking is interfered with, or spoilt – often by incompetence – we say someone has *gummed up the works*.

GYM The ancient Greeks trained and competed naked and our word *gymnasium* is based on the Greek *gumnazo* – meaning to train naked. But the roots of the term *gymkhana* were born in India when the British blended 'gym' with the Hindi *gendkhana*, meaning ball house or racquet court. This new term described an exercise ground for equestrian skills and training rather than the competitive event it has now come to mean.

H

HANDLE In the days of the American frontiersmen the pioneers frequently carried a supply of axe heads with them and whittled handles for them as and when required. Very often the iron heads were ill-fitted and flew off when struck hard against a tree, frequently causing injury to the axe man or others, with resultant upset. Sudden flare-ups of anger thus became known as *flying off the handle.*

HARBINGER More often used to denote a herald of bad news rather than good, *harbinger* was originally a title given to an officer who preceded an army to arrange lodgings and provisions. The modern usage of the word arose from the fear that when a harbinger arrived in the town the locals were about to be lumbered with a load of soldiers who had every intention of moving on without paying.

HASSLE In the American South the agitated breathing of hounds after a long run or a fight is called *hassle*, hence the word's current usage. When the dogs are restless they are quietened down by being thrown sweet, fried cornmeal, known as 'hush puppies'. In 1958 the Wolverine Shoe & Tanning Corporation of Michigan began marketing extremely comfortable (and comforting) pigskin shoes called Hush Puppies.

HAT In the 19th century it was occasionally the practice in the USA to signal the start of a fight or a race by dropping a hat. The quick response to this signal found its way into our language to indicate a person ready to do something at the first mention, or *at the drop of a hat*.

HATCHET In America in the 17th century, Samuel Sewall attended a meeting with Indian chiefs. They reached agreement and 'buried two axes in the ground, which ceremony to them is more significant and binding than all the Articles of Peace, the hatchet being their principal weapon'. Today we use the term *bury the hatchet* when we agree to end a dispute.

HAYWIRE Bundling-up bales of hay requires very tightly stretched wire. Should the wire snap there is an awful mess of hay and pieces of wire – the bale has gone *haywire*.

HEART If a damsel became enamoured with a knight she would sometimes favour him by handing him an article of her clothing – usually a scarf. If he then entered the jousting field to compete as her champion he would tie this scarf above his right elbow, thus *wearing his heart on his sleeve.*

Certain drinks are said to *warm the cockles of your heart.* This is derived from the resemblance – totally inaccurate – of the shape of the heart as depicted on lovers' cards to two cockle shells placed together.

HELL In Norse mythology the tormented dead roamed the domain of the Goddess Hel who, with packs of hounds, hunted down their souls. Hence, to be pursued by *the hounds of hell.*

In the so-called days of Merrie England lesser transgressions, not warranting capital punishment, might require the miscreant to stand in boiling water, the depth of which was directly proportional to the nature of his crime. Hence *through hell and high water* and also, when in some sort of trouble, *in hot water.*

HOBSON'S CHOICE In the 17th century Tobias Hobson ran a livery stable in Cambridge, England, where he rented out horses. He is said to have enforced a rule that the customer had to take the horse nearest the stable door rather than any particular mount he might want. Thus, when we have no choice at all we talk of *Hobson's choice.*

HOLLOW In the 17th century the word 'hollow' also meant thoroughly or completely and was derived from 'wholly'. This makes sense of the saying *to beat them hollow.*

HONEYMOON In Celtic times it was the custom for the families of newlyweds to stay with them for the first twenty-eight days of their married life, to ensure they settled in well together. During this time the couple were plied with a concoction of wine, herbs and honey – doubtless to keep up their strength! A similar drink, called mead, is still available in Cornwall, England. As twenty-eight days is the period of the moon's cycle, and the couple were enjoying a honey drink, we get *honeymoon.*

HOOK Under medieval English laws regulating the king's forests, people were allowed to pick up the wood that had fallen to the ground and cut down such dead branches as could be removed *by hook or by crook* – that is, a reaper's hook or a shepherd's crook. The modern usage of the phrase refers to doing or obtaining something by any means, fair or foul.

In the American Civil War General Joseph Hooker was very popular amongst his troops. But at his headquarters in Washington he became renowned for his heavy drinking and importation of prostitutes. As the number of troops increased the red-light district grew to meet the demand. The soldiers nicknamed these women 'Hooker's Division' and, subsequently, they became known as *hookers*.

HOOLIGAN In the late 19th century an Irish family living in the Southwark district of London were notorious for their riotous misbehaviour. Their surname was Houlihan which, when slightly altered by usage to hooligan, became a byword for trouble-making.

HORSE The age of a horse is determined by looking at its teeth. If you were given a horse it would be very impolite *to look a gift horse in the mouth*.

You can tell the age of a horse accurately by looking at its teeth. The pairs of permanent teeth appear in succession at definite ages. From a believable source we can accept what we see. The information comes *straight from the horse's mouth*. People full of their own importance are said to *get on their high horse*. This is a direct reference to the aristocracy riding tall thoroughbreds, whilst lesser mortals rode about on smaller, everyday horses called a 'hobby'.

HOTCH POTCH Originally 'hochepot', it described a stew with everything just thrown into the pot. In the past, meat and vegetables long past their best, and probably smelling pretty rank, were thrown together in a pot over an open fire by the poor. The French called this *pot-pourri* which meant 'putrid pot' – a bit different to today's sweet-smelling *potpourri*. And the expression *gone to pot*, meaning ruined or destroyed, originally referred to the meat cut into pieces for the pot.

HYSTERIA   The Greek word for womb was *hystera* (hence hysterectomy). In those days there was a strange belief that the womb was an unfixed organ that moved about in the abdomen. This movement upset women and produced *hysteria*.

By the way, in the Middle Ages the womb was often called 'The Mother' and, in this context, we get *mother-of-pearl*, the pearl being the womb of the oyster.

I, J

INOCULATION The first people to talk about inoculation were the gardeners of ancient Rome, whose usage was rather different from ours today. The term is based on *oculus*, Latin for the eye, or a bud; the verb *inoculare* described grafting a part of one plant onto another. In the 18th century the term acquired its medical application through the idea of introducing a foreign body into the patient.

INTOXICATED *Toxicon* is a Greek word meaning arrow poisoning – the tip of the arrow having been smeared with poison. From this we get the word *toxic*, and, following logically, *intoxicated* meaning drunk – or poisoned with alcohol.

JONES In 1913, when Arthur Momand started to produce cartoons for the New York *Globe* about a family dealing with daily problems to maintain a front, he initially called the series 'Keeping up with the Smiths'. But he quickly realised his immediate neighbours were Smiths and a lot of his cartoon incidents came close to their style of living. To avoid confrontation he changed the series to *Keeping up with the Joneses*.

JOURNEY Our ancestors were far less harried by demands on time and, in those days, a *journey* meant as far as one could travel in a day – usually around twenty miles. The name originates from the French for day, *jour*.

JUGGERNAUT An overpowering or gigantic force or object. In Hindu mythology the idol Jagannath (*jagat* World, *nathas* lord) represented the god Vishnu, and in the town of Puri a huge idol of Jagannath was annually dragged through the streets on a gigantic cart for worshippers to view and pray to. Because of the equally gigantic size of many modern-day transport vehicles passing along our roads they became known as *juggernauts*.

JUMBO A hundred years ago the most famous elephant of all times lived in London Zoo until he was sold to an American circus in 1882. His stuffed body is still on view in Boston, USA. His name was *Jumbo* and today the name is synonymous with anything extra large, be it packaging or the wide-bodied aircraft traversing our skies.

JUMPING ON THE BANDWAGON When it comes to canvassing for a political appointment, American politics has always been a rather show-biz affair. Before the advent of TV and mass media, candidates would often arrive in a town to drum up support parading through the streets on a wagon with a small band. Any local figure could climb onto the wagon to show his support for the candidate and hesitant locals would wait to see if the more prominent citizens joined the entourage before following suit and *jumping on the bandwagon*.

K

KETTLE In times gone by the Scots were want to throw elaborate parties on the banks of rivers. Marquees were pitched, drink flowed freely and big fires kindled. Large pots, or kettles, of boiling water hung over the fires and live salmon from the river was thrown into them. Drunken rowdiness was often the order of the day and then things frequently went wrong. If a boiling pot of fish was upset someone was bound to exclaim *that's a fine kettle of fish!*

KIDNAPPED A young goat is called a kid and as early as the 16th century it became a slang term for a child. If a child was stolen it has been 'kidnabbed' – nabbing meaning 'to grab hold of'. Since then usage of the word devolved into *kidnapped*.

KISS In the Middle Ages most people were illiterate, but they still had to sign documents. They made their mark with a cross which they then kissed to affirm their sincerity, in the same way that they kissed the Bible when taking an oath. This became the origin of an X for kisses at the end of a letter.

KNUCKLE In the 17th century the game of marbles was not only very popular, but taken seriously and bound by a number of rules. One of these was that the player must shoot directly from the spot where his marble landed. To do this he had to put his knuckles on the spot and then concentrate hard over his next shot. He had to *knuckle down* to the job in hand.

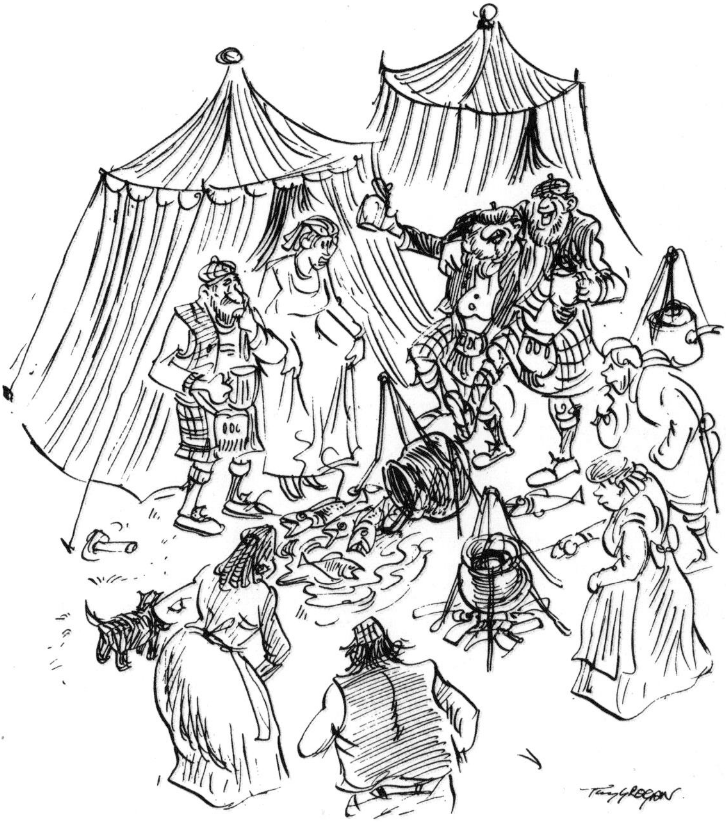

L

LADY Many ladies will doubtless be upset to learn that the word originally came from Old English to mean 'bread-kneader'. In those days their place was in the kitchen. However, do not lose heart, because 'lord' originally meant 'a keeper of the loaves'!

LAVATORY Originally the word *lavatory* had nothing whatsoever to do with – well, whatever you now associate it with! It was a 'place where you wash yourself' and in the cloisters of Gloucester Cathedral in England you can see a lavatorium – a monk's wash place. The word is from *lavare*, the Latin verb 'to wash'.

LEAF Many ancient manuscripts were written on palm leaves and other suitable leaves. Upon the invention of paper, pages were called 'leaves'. For the past 500 years, if a person wanted to start again and mend his ways it would be likened to going to a blank page in a notebook and beginning work afresh. Thus he would *turn over a new leaf*.

LETHARGY In Greek and Roman mythology the river Lethe was an underworld water that held the power to cause anyone who drank from it to forget his past life and become *lethargic*.

LETTUCE Cut this popular salad green and you will see some milky fluid. It is from this fluid that the vegetable got its name. In Latin it was known as *lactuca*, the 'milky plant' and in the French *laiteus*.

LEVIS This brand name for denim jeans is named after an

American sailmaker, Levi Strauss, who began the first manufacture of these trousers in 1869, The word 'jeans' itself is a corruption of the medieval French J. Jene or Janne, and the Latin Janua, all of which referred to the city of Genoa where the strong cotton material was woven.

LIE DETECTOR The first lie detector method, a long time before technology took over, originated in India. Suspects were sent into a darkened room where an ass was stabled, and were told to pull the animal's tail. If it brayed this was said to be an indication of guilt. However, the donkey's tail had also been dusted with black powder. Suspects with a clear conscience pulled the tail, those with something on their minds did not. A simple inspection of hands was carried out and revealed those with a guilty conscience.

LOCK, STOCK AND BARREL When gentlemen of old went hunting their bearers had to bring along the various components of the weapon. A stock, to which the barrel was affixed, and a lock – the firing mechanism. It might be a flintlock, matchlock or firelock – but always a lock. Leave behind one of these items and the day's hunting was ruined, so it was necessary completely to assemble the weapon *lock, stock and barrel*. The phrase is now often used to mean the entirety of something.

LOGGERHEADS A lot of sayings come from historic maritime practices. In the 1600s naval battles were often fought out on a hand-to-hand basis. A favourite weapon was a heavy ball of iron attached to a chain and a long handle. These were called 'loggerheads' and from this, of course, is derived the term to be *at loggerheads* with someone.

More naval terminology that we all use: In times past a ship's anchor was of a fairly basic design, shaped like a hook. The hook part was known as a 'fluke'. It often took quite a few heavings of the anchor until the crew were fortunate enough to secure a good hold, hence *lucky fluke*.

Rope featured in a big way in the days of sail and often a

sailor with no specific duty – or even off-duty – would sit on the deck mending ropes that had frayed at the ends. He was *at a loose end.*

M

MAD AS A HATTER   Zany. Daft. The Mad Hatter is a memorable character in Lewis Carroll's *Alice in Wonderland*, but the expression is much older. It derives from the effect on felt workers of the mercury once used in making felt hats. After some years many of them developed a tendency to twitch severely and behave abnormally.

MAGAZINE   was originally an Arabic word meaning a storehouse. It was brought into the English language in the 16th century and came to have the same meaning. In later years it especially applied to explosives and ammunition stores.

When periodicals started to be published they were also called *magazines*, because they were storehouses of articles, stories, information, etc.

MAKE THE GRADE   The steam railroad locomotive of early years frequently struggled to haul its heavy load up a steep gradient, but having finally got to the top it had achieved its object and *made the grade*.

MAYONNAISE   After the Duc de Richelieu had captured the port of Mahon in Minorca in 1756, he ordered his chef to prepare a celebratory banquet. Food supplies were running low and the chef had to make do with some pretty third-rate stuff. To disguise the somewhat doubtful flavour he concocted a sauce, which so impressed the Duc that he promptly named it after his victory, Mahonaise – now, of course, *mayonnaise*.

MILLINER   In the early 16th century Milan was one of the great fashion centres of the world – as it is today – and set styles for all of Europe. Gloves, hats, lace, ribbons, needles and jewellery were among the many items imported to England. Some of the traders of Milan set up shops in England and were known as 'Milaners'. Many small shops specialised in making and selling ladies' hats and the English pronounced Milaners as *milliners* and to this day the word is associated exclusively with the designers and makers of ladies' hats.

MOANING MINNIE During World War II the Germans used a multi-barrelled mine-thrower they called a *Minenwerfer*. Allied troops ducked when they heard the distinctive sound of the mortars heading their way and nicknamed the machine *Moaning Minnie* which, carried into civvy street, came to describe any habitual whinger.

MONEY In the past, when ships docked in the major ports in England, seamen used to sell lengths of old rope on the quayside to raise money for food and drink. They got *money for old rope*.

MONTHS OF THE YEAR We have the ancient Romans to thank for our calendar.
January: From Janus, the Roman god of doors and beginnings, who had two faces, one looking forward and one backward. The Latin for door is *janua*. From this we get *janitor*, a doorkeeper.
February: This was the month when the Romans practised religious rites of purification. The Roman Catholic Church celebrates the Purification of the Virgin Mary on the 2nd. The Latin word *februare* means 'to purify'.
March: Named for Mars, the God of War. The Romans honoured Mars, whom they called *Martius*.
April: There are two accepted origins for the name of this month: one from the Latin *aperire*, to open, because it is the month in the Northern Hemisphere when the buds of flowers and trees open out. The other possible origin is that April

is connected with the Greek Goddess of Love, Aphrodite, because it is the time of the year when young people traditionally turn their thoughts to love.

May: In honour of the Roman goddess Maia, who signified Spring.

June: From the Roman goddess Juno.

July: Originally known as *Quintilis*, this was the month in which Julius Caesar was born. After Caesar was assassinated Mark Antony changed *Quintilis* to July in his honour.

August: Another month associated with the Caesar family. The Roman emperor Augustus Caesar was the grand-nephew of Julius Caesar. Although born in September, most of the great successes attributed to Augustus were achieved in this month, so it was considered appropriate to name August after him. It was also conveniently next to the month named after his great-uncle.

September: Derived from the Latin *septus*, which means seven. In the ancient Roman calendar this was the seventh month.

October: For the same reasons as September, this was then the eighth month of the Roman calendar and comes from the Latin *octo*, or eight.

November: On the same theme, the Latin *novem* means nine.

December: You've guessed it! Back to the first Roman calendar which originally had only ten months. *Decem* is Latin for ten.

MOON Why do we say something happens *once in a blue moon*? The appearance of a blue moon is a rarity and usually occurs when a large volcanic eruption or an extensive forest fire throws dust particles high in the atmosphere. These particles can be of many colours, but whilst other colours are reflected, blue is absorbed and the moon appears to be blue.

MUD Before the start of an 18th-century cross-country horse race, a stirrup cup would be drunk and competitors toasted each other. If one rider thought he would lead the race throughout – and this meant that every other rider would be splattered by the mud kicked up by his mount – he would boastfully say *here's mud in your eye*.

MUMBO JUMBO   To the Mandingo people of Senegal, 'Mama Dyumbo' was a god of punishment. When they wished to bring retribution upon someone they would dance furiously and call upon the god to act against the enemy. Early explorers, knowing of the god but not understanding the language of the tribe, soon corrupted the god's name to *mumbo jumbo*.

MUSTARD   In Latin, new or unmatured wine was known as *mustus* and made an ideal base for mixing hot spices into the paste which we now know as *mustard*.

N, O

NEWS We talk freely of news put out by all sections of the media, but where does the word come from? One theory that seems perfectly feasible is that 'news' comes from all four corners of the world – *north, east, west,* and *south.* Got it?

NIGHTMARE In Old English the word 'mare' referred to a kind of female monster believed to sit on your chest whilst you slept and gave you bad dreams. Hence *nightmare.*

NINE-DAY WONDER Monks of old offered to help the wrong-doer to heaven by selling him a 'novena'. For this money the sinner was assured that the monk would pray for him for nine days. In the eyes of practical people this was a little suspect and became known as a *nine-day wonder*.

NOSE The human nose has always been associated with an inquisitive nature. Witness *sticking his nose into someone else's business*. The Archbishop of Canterbury in the reign of Queen Elizabeth I was one Matthew Parker. He became very unpopular because of his constant prying into the behaviour of his priests and how they ran their diocese and earned the unflattering name *nosey Parker*.

NUTSHELL If something is *put in a nutshell*, it is brief and concise. Nearly 2 000 years ago, Homer's *Iliad* had been copied in such a minute script that the entire work could be contained in a walnut shell. In 1590, Peter Bales in England actually wrote a Bible small enough to go into a walnut shell.

OSTRACISE The Athenians did not allow the public to vote at election time. This was done by other politicians. But the public did have a way to get rid of a politician who displeased them. If they could raise more than 10 000 votes of disfavour, he was banished from the city and all his property and wealth confiscated. These votes were cast on a little piece of tile or shell, known in Greek as an *ostrakon*, hence the modern use of *ostracise*.

And, as would seem to be the case nowadays, the politician's regard for the public's brainpower was pretty low. A member of the public holding no civic responsibility was called by the Greeks *idiotes* and survives today as *idiot*.

P, Q

P'S AND Q'S Back in the 1700s it became the custom of regulars at an inn to 'keep a tab'. Against the customer's name the landlord would chalk a 'P' for a pint and a 'Q' for a quart of ale. Sometimes it was necessary for the publican to be reminded to *mind his P's and Q's*. When the customer eventually pays the outstanding account he has *settled an old score* and *wiped the slate clean*.

PALACE The luxurious homes of Roman emperors were built on the Palatine Hill – then called the 'Palatium' – one of the seven hills of Rome. *Palaces* can thus be said to take their name from this Roman hill.

PAN The 1849 Gold Rush produced many expressions used to this day. Something good is said to *pan out*, which is a reference to sifting the gold particles from the dross. The gold extracted from the mud was called *pay dirt*, now used to describe striking any profitable enterprise.

But to *pay through the nose* was – and is – to be charged an exorbitant price. The expression stems way back to the ninth century when the Danes levied a tax on the Irish. Anyone failing to pay the tax was punished by having his nose slit.

PANIC The Greek god Pan had the ability to frighten everyone in the countryside, which was his domain and from this we get *panic*. The term *to hit the panic button* is very recent and comes from World War II, when American bomber pilots pressed a red button to alert all crew to bale out.

PANTRY In Old French 'paneterie' meant a 'bread closet'. Hence our present-day *pantry*. Similarly, a larder means much the same thing as a pantry, but in bygone days it was where you kept your lard (pork fat or fatty bacon). So, in those days, you had one room to store your bread and another to store your lard.

PARTING SHOT The Parthians of Asia were highly skilled horsemen, able to fire their bows to the rear whilst at full gallop. One of their tricks during battle was to feign disarrayed retreat and invariably their adversaries would pursue them, sensing victory. Once out in the open the Parthians would turn, fire and cut their pursuers to smithereens. This became known as a 'Parthian shot' and has become, in modern times, a *parting shot,* or insult, delivered on taking one's leave.

PASSING THE BUCK On the poker tables of the American West they kept a piece of heavy-gauge buckshot. As soon as a player picked up the cards to deal, he moved the marker to his left, thus *passing the buck,* or responsibility, to the next man.

PATENT basically means to open out or to show. When a company takes out a patent it is declaring to all that it owns the rights. The first synthetic leathers emerged under such protection and therefore became known as *patent leather.*

PEG In Saxon times ale-drinking contests were popular amongst young warriors. Long cattle horns – the forerunner of the Yard of Ale – would have measuring pegs inserted in them and the horn filled with ale to a given measure. This had to be quaffed in one continuous swallow, without pause for breath. If a challenger came along and succeeded in drinking an even greater measure than the champion he was said to have *taken him down a peg or two.*

PENNY In 1855 the City of London built a number of public toilets, charging one penny entrance. This price remained the same until 1971 when decimalisation was introduced – thus creating a record for price stability. These coin-operated loos produced two phrases for the English language: *The penny has dropped* and *spend a penny*.

PETARD One of the earliest explosive devices used to breach castle walls or gates was called a petard. It got its name from the French *péter*, referring to a horse breaking wind! One can only assume this is how the bomb sounded when it exploded. But the device was notoriously unreliable and as often as not blew the soldier igniting it into the air, leaving him *hoisted with his own petard*.

PETER In the 19th-century mining industry, gunpowder was the main source for blasting. The essential ingredient of this explosive was salpetre and it became affectionately known as 'Peter'. When a mine had exhausted its potential it was said to have *petered out*. Indeed, when this happened, the blasters had got *down to bedrock* and the investment was *stony broke*!

PIG Fairgrounds of old have produced a number of today's sayings. One confidence trick was to sell a suckling pig. The dupe would be shown the pig in a sack – then known as a 'poke', short for pocket – which was put aside whilst they haggled over the price. This bit of sharp practice gave rise to the saying *buying a pig in a poke*. Once the purchase was agreed to the customer would be handed a different tied sack that contained either a cat or a puppy and a bit of ballast. Should the buyer inspect his wares there and then he literally *let the cat out of the bag* or found he had been *sold a pup*!

PIGGY BANKS are so named from the northern English dialect 'pigga', which meant the earthenware from which these items were first made.

PIPING HOT 'Piping' is the sound made by a whistle or musical pipe. When a nonelectric kettle boiled, it whistled, indicating that the water was *piping hot*.

PLUMBER   When you call for a *plumber* have you ever wondered why there is a 'b' in the spelling? It goes back to the days when all pipes used in plumbing were made of lead. The Latin for lead is *plumbum* and originally a plumber was a 'lead-worker'.

POLE-AXE   When we talk of a stunned person as being *pole-axed* this is a reference to the heavy axe once used to behead people. 'Poll' means head.

POODLE   Far from being French, the *poodle* is a German water dog, named from *pudeln* – to splash in water. The same German word produced our *puddle* and *pudding*. Misconception arose when the toy variety of the poodle became known as a 'French Poodle'. The Great Dane is German too, but the French believed it to be Danish.

PULL THE WOOL   To *pull the wool* over someone's eyes is to deceive them. The literal origin of the phrase goes back to the 19th century, when men commonly wore wool wigs. If you pulled one of them over the wearer's eyes, he would be unable to see what was going on.

The moment the snail encounters something threatening it retracts its tiny horns. This is why the aggressive person is sometimes told to *pull in his horns*.

PULLING HIS LEG   means to tease someone. But the origin of the expression, like so many we use today, is quite gruesome. Before hanging became a scientific art – the hangman skilled in working out the weight and length of drop required to guarantee a clean execution – relatives of the condemned were allowed to wait below the gallows to pull on the victim's legs in order to end his suffering as soon as possible.

R

RACK The rack used in medieval torture chambers comes from the Old Irish 'rikim' – to stretch. Thus, we *rack our brains* or, when under strain we are *nerve-racked*, and we suffer from *racking pain* or headaches. However, if something goes to *rack and ruin*, it's in a state of wreckage, the word 'wrack' being a variant of 'wreck'.

RACQUET Tennis as we know it today originated by knocking a ball about with the flat of the hand. The Arabic word *raha* means the flat of the hand and eventually gave us *racquet* or, now commonly, *racket*. In medieval England a form of tennis was played in courtyards, where natural obstacles such as columns and other supports heightened the excitement of the game, giving us the expression *from pillar to post*. Incidentally, the word tennis originated from the French *tenez!*, a court call meaning 'hold yourself ready to receive service'.

REAL McCOY In the late 19th century a boxer who fought under the name of 'Kid McCoy' was so good that other boxers adopted the name, whereupon he had to bill himself as 'the real McCoy', and so we get the expression to this day, meaning the genuine article.

RECIPE This familiar cookery term is pure Latin. Its literal meaning is 'take'; as in so many opening instructions for preparing a dish which start, for example, with 'take six eggs'...

RED A herring that is cured by smoking turns red. It also has a strong odour and in the 19th century hunting dogs were often trained to follow a scent by using a red herring that had been dragged along the ground. People opposed to hunting would sometimes drag a red herring across the trail of the fox and the dogs would give up the scent of the fox and follow that of the herring. Thus, a *red herring* is something to throw one off the track, a diversionary action.

A red-letter day is a memorable day or date. It comes from a custom that has endured from the 15th century of signifying holy days and days important to the Church by printing the numbers in red on the calendar.

RIDE ROUGHSHOD For country riding a horse obviously needed good footing, so not all the nails securing the horseshoe were driven fully home. Those left protruding were like an athlete's running spikes and this was known as 'roughshod'. Imagine, if you will, those hooves pounding over you and you will realise what it means to *ride roughshod* over somebody.

RINGLEADER In times past witches used to dance in rings, the head witch being the *ringleader*.

RIVAL Originally a *rival* was someone who drew water from the same stream as oneself. It comes from the Latin *rivus*, a river.

ROAM In medieval times pilgrimages were the in-thing. Europe teemed with the faithful journeying from shrine to shrine. Rome was their ultimate goal, but the pilgrims would plot their route there by taking in as many shrines as possible on the way. The name of their final destination described such wanderings, and this was gradually changed to *roam*.

ROME The city did not, in fact, get its name from Romulus, but the river Ruma, now the Tiber. One of the hills of ancient Rome was given over to the pagan soothsayers, who were known as 'Vaticinatores' – from 'vaticinia', a place of divination. This area is now the Papal State of the Vatican.

RULE OF THUMB   A rough measure or guide. The breadth of the knuckle of a man's thumb is approximately one inch and has often served as a measure when a more precise one was not available. The practice dates back to the 1600s.

S

SABOTAGE The sabot is a wooden clog that was once extensively worn by the French and Dutch peasantry. In the 19th and early 20th centuries, during revolts against harsh labour conditions, these peasants would take their sabots and thrust them into the factory machinery and *sabotage* it.

And in Victorian times in the north of England many male workers also wore wooden clogs. As a form of light entertainment, clog fights were staged whereby two men put their hands behind their backs and tried to kick hell out of each other's legs – hence *shindig*, now generally applied to a rowdy party.

SACK To *get the sack* is to be dismissed from one's job. It was once 'to get the bag', meaning to leave abruptly and was later applied to being fired. Roving workers carried their tools in a sack or bag and when the work was ended, or a man was dismissed, the worker picked up his sack and moved on.

And while on the topic of sacks, the *knapsack* takes its name from the Middle Dutch *cnappen*, to eat, because it once carried food for a journey. *Haversack* comes from the German *Habersack* – a sack of oats carried to provide food for a horse. Also German, *Rücken* means the back, giving meaning to *rucksack*, which is carried on the back.

SALT The Romans paid part of their soldiers' wages in salt, then a rare commodity. Thus, somebody who has proved himself and justified his cost is *worth his salt*. Later the soldiers were given money to buy salt. 'Salarium' is Latin for salt and from this we get *salary*.

SAPPER These days the word 'zap' is used to describe

killing. The Mafia are great at zapping and it is an Italian word by origin. Far from being a modern Americanism, it goes back to the 1600s and comes from the Italian *zappare* – to inflict damage by explosives. Thus, in English, the soldier who uses explosives is known as a *sapper*.

SCAPEGOAT In the past the ritual of the Jewish Day of Atonement required the priest to bring two goats before the altar of the tabernacle. By casting lots he selected one of them as an offering to Jehovah. The other was for Azazel – a demon that lived in the wilderness. The high priest transferred the sins of the people to this goat and allowed it to escape and go to Azazel. Abbreviation made it a *scapegoat*, now a person on whom blame unfairly falls.

SCOT-FREE Getting off *scot-free* is not an insult to the Scots. The term is derived from the old Norse *skot* – meaning a tax.

SCRATCH The expressions *starting from scratch* and *not coming up to scratch* have unpleasant origins. They come from the days of dog-fighting as a sport. When dogs were first put before their opponents in the ring they first had to scratch each other before going in for the kill. If a dog stopped during a fight it was taken back to the corner and had to *start from scratch*. If a dog refused to fight he was deemed as *not coming up to scratch*.

SHELL OUT At one time sea shells were used as measuring scoops. The trader using such a scoop was watched very closely and told to *shell out*. This allusion to shells also comes from the days when shells were used as currency. Today it means pay up.

SHIP In the days of sail merchant ships were slow and adverse winds affected schedules. Communication was also difficult. Many investors ashore had a financial interest in the cargo, and since it was uncertain when the ship would arrive, waited anxiously. Many were heard to say 'I'll be alright *when my ship comes in.*'

SHORT SHRIFT In former times a person condemned to death had little time to prepare for his fate. But there was a pretence at justice and he was allowed 'shrift'; that is, he was allowed to see a priest and confess his sins and purge his soul. But the executioners were impatient, wanted to get on with the job in hand, and only allowed the prisoner a very short time with the priest. Today, *short shrift* is used to mean curt or dismissive treatment of a person or an issue.

SIRLOIN One of the most enduring – and endearing – myths attached to beef is that *sirloin* derives its name from some old monarch who was so fond of loin of beef that he knighted it Sir Loin. In reality, the term is derived from the French 'sur loigne', meaning above the loin.

A number of people who believed the old story produced yet another culinary term. They called a double sirloin a *baron of beef*, since this is one step higher in the peerage than a knight.

SLAP-BANG   In the doss houses of yesteryear vagrants called the meal room a *slap-bang*. You slapped down your money and a plateful of that day's fare was banged down in front of you. Today we use the term to describe doing something in a rough and ready way, totally lacking finesse.

SLUSH FUND   In the old sailing days, the fat from the boiling down of any fresh meat brought on board at the last port, together with that which sealed the pork barrels, was stored by the ship's cook. The mushy fat thus produced was known as 'slush' and was a perk for the cook and the purser, who made candles from it for sale ashore. The two men then shared the *slush fund*, nowadays something put away for emergencies, or for use as a bribe.

SNOB   A somewhat arrogant person with social or intellectual pretensions, who looks down on those he considers inferior. In the early days of Oxford and Cambridge Universities, students not only had to register their names, but their rank. Those of noble birth had to log their title and those of lesser station were obliged to put *sine nobilitae*, Latin for 'without nobility'. This was later abbreviated to 'snob' and used by the titled students to describe those of lower status.

SOCK   In 1877 the forerunner of the present sophisticated music centre was invented and called a 'phonograph'. The first models had no volume control and listeners often shoved a sock into the big horn to mute the sound. Others often demanded that they *put a sock in it*!

SOLVENT   The word *solvent*, meaning something which can dissolve other substances, comes from the Latin *solvere* – meaning to loosen or detach. When it is used in a financial sense solvent applies to people or companies with enough money to lose their debts. The same connotation has given us *solution* – as in losing a problem. A relative is *absolution*, which results in sinners being freed of their sins.

SOS The Morse Code distress signal *SOS* (dot-dot-dot- – dash-dash-dash – dot-dot-dot) does not stand for 'Save Our Souls' and was never intended to. It was chosen because it was eminently suitable for remembering in times of great stress and would probably be known even by a novice, such as a ship's passenger. It is transmitted as a pattern, not as a sequence of letters.

SPENDTHRIFT Something of a contradiction in terms, since one either spends or is thrifty! Originally it was called a 'wastethrift' and the Prodigal Son was a prime example.

SPITTING IMAGE Amongst black Americans in the deep South the son of a father who had passed away and was very much like his late father was said to be the 'spirit and image' of his father, but years of dialect reduced this to *spitting image*.

STEEPLECHASE Because church steeples stood out above surrounding buildings in times past they were used as landmarks. In Ireland it became popular to hold horse races using the steeples as starting and finishing points, hence *steeplechase*.

SWAN SONG A farewell; one's last appearance, performance or composition. The swan does not sing, but legend has it that a dying swan at last manages to give voice before passing away.

SWEATER In the 19th century the heavy blanket thrown over a horse to make it sweat off some weight before a race was called a *sweater*. Then athletes took to wearing heavy flannel wear for the same reason. The sports fashion business is nothing new and upper-body woollen sweating garments were soon being worn by people who never went near a track. So, to this day, it remains a *sweater*. A *jumper*, however, has nothing to do with sport. It derives from the French word *jupe*, which means a skirt. Originally a jumper was a long cotton shirt-like garment worn by sailors, or the smock worn by yokels. When these became woollen and shorter the name remained.

SWORD In classical mythology Damocles was a courtier in the reign of Dionysius I of Syracuse in the fifth century B.C. He was overeffusive in his praise of his ruler's power and happiness. Dionysius wanted to show him that power and happiness are precarious, so he gave Damocles a magnificent banquet. Damocles presumably enjoyed it until he looked up; over his head was an unsheathed sword suspended by a single hair. Thus, when under threat, we nowadays talk of the *sword of Damocles* hanging over us or, when holding on to safety, *hanging by a thread*.

T

TALLY Many years ago, records of points in games were kept by scratching – or scoring – lines on a stick called a *tally*, which comes from the French *tailler*, meaning to cut. We still *keep a tally*, or record of accounts, and in games, we keep a *score* for similar reasons.

On the old tally sticks the end of a game was indicated by a special notch, which has also given us *in the nick of time*.

TANK Why is an army tank so called? During World War I these leviathans, that had such a psychological impact on the enemy, had to be transported in secret. So they were shipped in massive wooden crates labelled 'Bulk Water Carriers'. Since the origins of the word itself refer to anything containing or storing water, the vehicles were nicknamed "tanks" and the name stuck.

TANTRUM Simple spinning toys have long been popular with children. Those that were thrown from a loop of string were called 'tantrums', based on the whirling dance called the tarantella. *Tantrum* later came to mean a bout of temper – an allusion to the top spinning out of control. When a spinning toy reaches a certain speed it appears motionless and is said to sleep. Hence *sleep like a top*.

TANTALISE According to Greek legend, Tantalus, the son of Zeus, was punished for his crimes by having to stand up to his chin in water, with fruit hanging over his head. He was desperately hungry and thirsty, but the fruit was pulled away from him when he looked up and the waters receded when he stooped to drink. Thus we are *tantalised* by something inaccessible which we desire.

TAR Sheep cannot be branded, it would spoil the fleece and, in any case, after the first season the wool would conceal the brand. So sheep are daubed in various distinguishing ways and formerly tar was the most common substance used. So those *tarred with the same brush* belonged to the same flock.

Incidentally, the saying 'the ship was lost for a pennyworth of tar' originally applied to 'the sheep was lost . . .'

TATTOO In the mid-17th century English troops occupied parts of the Netherlands. The Dutch civilians were understandably hostile to these soldiers, and the military authorities devised a system whereby, at 9 pm, a drum squad marched through the streets playing a distinctive beat to order soldiers to leave the taverns, fall in behind the drummers and march back to barracks. The Dutch called this *taptoe*, meaning 'the (beer) tap is shut'. The troops corrupted this word to *tattoo*. To this day military extravaganzas open and close with this traditional tattoo beat.

As for the other tattoo; this bodily graffiti got its name from the Polynesian *tatu*, meaning a mark or design. It started with Captain Cook's crew in Tahiti.

TAWDRY In Cambridgeshire there used to be an annual fair on the Isle of Ely in honour of St Audrey. Traditionally this was a market for some of the finest lace products, but the fair began to lose its renown with the introduction of cheap trash. Such merchandise earned a corruption of the saint's name and was labelled as *tawdry*.

TAXI In 1911 one of the first airfields in Britain was Brooklands in Surrey. There, an old broken-down monoplane was used for training pilots on the ground. It was known by all students as the 'taxi'. Eventually this spread to trainer aircraft at other flying schools used for motion on the ground. Thus, to this day, aircraft *taxi* out to the runway.

TENTERHOOKS A 'tenter' was a wooden frame used to stretch cloth during its manufacture. The cloth was fastened to the frame by hooks called 'tenterhooks'. So, if you are *on tenterhooks* you are being stretched taut by suspense.

TEDDY BEAR When President Theodore ('Teddy') Roosevelt was hunting in Mississippi in 1902 his heart went out to a little bear cub he found abondoned and he arranged for its safekeeping. The story hit all the newspapers and a Brooklyn shopkeeper and his wife started to make stuffed toy bears. They got permission from the President to call them *teddy bears*.

THIMBLE It takes its name from the thumb on which it was worn. Originally it was called a 'thumb bell' and cobblers and saddlers used it to push needles through leather.

TOADY At fairgrounds the medicine man was a great draw. But somewhere in the crowd of onlookers an assistant was planted. The toad in those days was believed to be lethal and this aide would come forward – apparently as a volunteer – to eat a piece of the toad's meat to prove the miraculous value of the medicine offered. He was known as a *toady* – an expression we know today to mean anyone who behaves in a servile manner or fawns upon someone, especially the boss! However, the remedy, eagerly bought by the crowd, often created more ills than it cured. Sometimes the whole village would set off in pursuit of the good 'doctor' and force him to drink several bottles of his own brew, thus giving him *a dose of his own medicine*.

TOAST Drinking a toast has grown out of an old custom of adding flavour to a glass of wine by putting a piece of spiced toast into the glass. In Shakespeare's *The Merry Wives of Windsor* Falstaff commanded, 'Fetch me a quart of sack – and put a toast in 't.'

TROPHY In ancient times, when the Greeks put the enemy to flight and won the battle they would erect a monument made of captured weapons. This was called a *trope*, meaning to put to flight, and is the source of our present-day *trophy*.

TRUTH An old fable has it that Truth and Falsehood went for a swim together, leaving their clothes on shore. Falsehood came out of the water first and put on Truth's clothes. Truth, refusing to don the clothes of Falsehood, went naked. *Naked truth.*

U, V

UNDER Passengers prone to seasickness when the ship meets rough water tend to go below deck to a central point of the vessel, where the motion is at a minimum and out of the wind and rain. They are then said to be *under the weather*, a term we use on dry land to mean anyone feeling unwell.

In the 16th century card players were deft at holding extra cards under their hands. This kind of cheating gave rise to *underhand*, which we now use to describe any sly or deceitful action.

VACCINE During the 18th century it was discovered that milkmaids who caught cowpox from cows became immune from the usually fatal smallpox. Cowpox is a mild form of smallpox. It was proposed that persons be inoculated with the cowpox virus. As the Latin for cow is *vacca* this virus was called *vaccine* and the actual inoculation *vaccination*.

VALENTINE In ancient Rome the Feast of Lupercalia, basically a mating ceremony to mop up unmarried persons, was celebrated on 15 February. The names of all girls of marriageable age were placed in an urn and the men drew lots to see who they would get. The ritual came to England with the Romans, but when it evolved into something little short of an orgy, the Church stepped in. It was reduced to the simple exchange of love tokens and the feast date was moved back to the nearest saint's day which happened to be 14 February and that of two saints named *Valentine*.

VILLAIN didn't originally mean a lawbreaker. In Roman times farm labourers were called 'villains' because the master's villa was the central point on the land where they toiled.

W, Y

WAKE As we all know, there are many beliefs and superstitions surrounding death. People once believed that the spirit of the deceased would try and take over the body of one of the family. The only way to prevent this was constant vigilance. Hence the *wake*, when everyone quite literally stayed awake and alert. To confuse the would-be invader, all present dressed in black, even blackening their faces, so that the spirit would not be able to tell one from another.

When the coffin was placed in the grave a heavy stone was dropped on top as an additional precaution and yet another placed on the filled-in grave. This last gradually became the tombstone, or headstone we know today.

WATERLOO It was at Waterloo in Belgium that Napoleon and his forces were soundly defeated in 1815 by British and Prussian forces under the Duke of Wellington and Marshal Blucher. Napoleon had so dominated Europe for more than a decade that the name of the memorable battle has remained in the language to signify a severe defeat or obstacle that cannot be overcome, with the expression *to meet one's Waterloo*.

WEST The notorious Tyburn gibbet in London stood on the site where Marble Arch now stands. This was well west of the City of London and when a prisoner was transported in the tumbril for execution by hanging, he was said to have *gone west*.

WET BEHIND THE EARS Innocent, naive. The allusion is to the newborn farm animal – a calf for example – that comes into the world wet all over and dries last in the small indentation behind the ears. If you are young enough to be still wet behind the ears you have had little experience of life.

WHITE ELEPHANT A possession that is sometimes more of a problem than a pleasure. A useless item – sometimes quite valuable – that one cannot easily get rid of. Legend has it that rare albino elephants in ancient Siam automatically became the property of the king. If a courtier fell out of favour the king would give him a white elephant and the courtier would soon be ruined by the cost of keeping the animal.

WHISTLE Wishful thinking will often cause someone to advise that *you can whistle for it*. This comes from the days of sail. When a ship was becalmed the crew believed that if they gathered together on deck and whistled this would raise the wind. Needless to say, this was a forlorn hope. Another saying, less used but from the same origin, is *whistling in the wind*.

WINDOW The ancient Norse people built dwellings with one or two apertures in the walls to allow the circulation of fresh air. Their word for these was *vindrauga – vindr* meaning wind and *auga* an eye. Literally the 'wind's eye'. From this we derive our word *window*. It wasn't until the Middle Ages that glass was put into these apertures.

WOOD Our ancestors worshipped trees, believing them to be the dwelling places of deities and spirits. If someone needed help in a venture he would go to the forest, select the tree where the required god dwelled, put his hands on the trunk and make his request. *Touch wood*!

WORSHIP When you *worship* God you are really considering God's 'worth'. You are giving praise to His 'worth=ship', or worthiness. This makes sense of civil titles like 'His Worship the Mayor'.

YANKEE   Before the American Revolution the English used to refer to a sailor from New England contemptuously as a 'Little John'. These sailors were of Dutch origin and 'Little John' was a corruption of the Dutch diminutive for Jan – Janke. This was soon anglicised to *Yankee* and its abbreviation, *Yank*.

The Americans, in turn, liked to call the British *Limeys*. This goes back to the days of long voyages under sail when British sailors were given daily tots of lime juice to prevent scurvy.